LAST TRAIN TO WISDOM

Lesson from fifty great

Author: Mohammad Adeeb

the Most Influential
Persons in History "
without order "

❖ **Jeff bozos**

❖ **Nelson Mandela**

❖ **Napoleon Bonaparte**

❖ **Che Guevara**

❖**Fidel Castro**

- **Yasser arafat**

- Julius caesar

- **Alfred Nobel**

- Ernest Hemingway

- William Shakespeare

- Pablo Picasso

- Marie Curie

- ❖ **Johann Wolfgang von Goethe**

- ❖ **Salvador Dali**

- ❖ **Jean-Jacques Rousseau**

- ❖ **Ludwig van Beethoven**

- ❖ **Adolf Hitler**
- ❖ **Benito Mussolini**

- ❖ **Saddam hussein**

- ❖ **Joseph Stalin**

- ❖ **Leonardo da Vinci**

- ❖ **Friedrich Nietzsche**

- ❖ **Charlie Chaplin**

- ❖ **Henry ford**

- ❖ **George Washington**

- ❖ **Aristotle**

- ❖ Martin Luther

- ❖ **the Wright Brothers**

- ❖ Thomas Edison

- ❖ **Plato**

- ❖ Alexander Graham Bell

- ❖ Imam " ali ibn abi taleb "

- ❖ **uthman ibn affan**

- ❖ **Umar Ibn Al-Khattab**

- ❖ **Abu baker siddiq**

1-Jeff Bezos : He is the founder, CEO, and president of Amazon.com

9

Jeff Bezos Quotes

- *One of the things that I hope will distinguish*

Amazon.com is that we continue to be a company that defies easy analogy. This requires a lot of innovation, and innovation requires a lot of random walks.

- *"The best customer service is if the customer doesn't need to call you, doesn't need to talk to you. It just works." – Jeff Bezos Quotes*

- *"Put the customer first. Invent. And be patient." Jeff Bezos Quotes*

- *"In business, what's dangerous is not to evolve."*

- *"The common question that gets asked in business is, 'why?' That's a good question, but an equally valid question is, 'why not?'"*

- *"If you do build a great experience, customers tell each other about that. Word of mouth is very powerful."*

- *"Patience, persistence, and obsessive attention to detail."*

- *"A company shouldn't get addicted to being shiny because shiny doesn't last."*

- *"There are two kinds of companies, those that work to try to charge more and those that work to charge less. We will be the second."*

- *"If you do build a great experience, customers*

13

*tell each other about
that. Word of mouth is
very powerful."*

- *"A brand for a company
  is like a reputation for a
  person. You earn
  reputation by trying to do
  hard things well."*

- *"When the world
  changes around you and
  when it changes against
  you, what used to be a
  tail wind is now a
  headwind, you have to
  lean into that and figure*

out what to do because complaining isn't a strategy."

- *"Obsess about customers, not competitors."*

- *"Now, Amazon sells almost anything we can imagine, no matter the season. Thanks to e-commerce, it's never too early to shop for holidays like Halloween and Christmas. From sites specially meant for makeup, practical furniture, personalized or unique trinkets, and colorful child-friendly accessories, Amazon remains an inspiration and the standard for other e-commerce businesses worldwide."*

- *"You don't want to negotiate the price of simple things you buy every day."*

- *"The people who are right a lot, often change their minds."*

- _"My view is there's no bad time to Innovate"_

- _"Your brand is what other people say about you when you're not in the room."_

- _"A company shouldn't get addicted to being shiny, because shiny doesn't last."_

- _"All businesses need to be forever."_

- _"We expect all our businesses to have a positive impact on our_ *top and bottom lines. Profitability is very important to us or we wouldn't be in this business."*

- *"Part of company culture is path-dependent – it's the lessons you learn along the way." – Jeff Bezos Quotes*

- *"No business can continue to shrink. That can only go on for so long before irrelevancy sets in."*

- *"We have focused like a laser on customer experience, and that really does matter."*

- *"Life is too short to hang out with people who are not resourceful"*

- *"People who are right most of the time are people who change their minds often."*

- *"If you can't tolerate critics, don't do anything new or interesting."*

19

- *"One of the huge mistakes people make is that they try to force an interest on themselves. You don't choose your passion; your passion chooses you."*

- *"It's hard to find things that won't sell online."*

- *"We can't be in survival mode. We have to be in growth mode."*

- *"This has the potential to be bigger than anything we've ever done."*

- *"If you decide that you're going to do only the things you know are going to work, you're going to leave a lot of opportunity on the table."*

- *"Be stubborn on vision, but flexible on details."*

- *"I don't want to use my creative energy on somebody else's user interface."*

- *"There'll always be serendipity involved in the discovery."*

- *"I knew that if I failed I wouldn't regret that, but I knew the one thing I might regret is not trying."*

- *"If you double the number of experiments you do per year you're going to double your inventiveness."*

- *"It's not an experiment if you know it's going to work."*

- *"If you're not stubborn, you'll give up on experiments too soon. And if you're not flexible, you'll pound your head against the wall and you won't see a different solution to a problem you're trying to solve."*

- *"The thing that motivates me is a very common form of motivation. And that is, with other folks counting on me, it's so easy to be motivated."*

- *"Profitability is very important to us or we*

wouldn't be in this
business."

- "Cleverness is a gift,
kindness is a choice."

- "The death knell for any
enterprise is to glorify
the past — no matter
how good it was."

- "The human brain is an
incredible pattern-
matching machine."

- "You have to be willing
to be misunderstood if

you're going to innovate."

- *"Invention is by its very nature disruptive. If you want to be understood at all times, then don't do anything new."*

- *"You know, we love stories and we love narrative; we love to get lost in an author's world."*

- *"I wanted a woman who could get me out of a Third World prison. Life's too short to hang out*

2- Nelson Mandela

**Former President of South
Africa**

- *It always seems
impossible until it's done.*

- *Education is the most powerful weapon which you can use to change the world.*

- *There is no passion to be found playing small - in settling for a life that is less than the one you are capable of living.*

- *I learned that courage was not the absence of fear, but the triumph over it. The brave man is not he who does not feel afraid, but he who conquers that fear.*

- *A good head and a good heart are always a formidable combination.*

- *For to be free is not merely to cast off one's chains, but to live in a way that respects and enhances the freedom of others.*

- *The greatest glory in living lies not in never falling, but in rising every time we fall.*

- *And as we let our own light shine, we*

unconsciously give other people permission to do the same

- *After climbing a great hill, one only finds that there are many more hills to climb.*

- *If you talk to a man in a language he understands, that goes to his head. If you talk to him in his language, that goes to his heart*
3-Napoleon Bonaparte quote

- *Religion is what keeps the poor from murdering the rich.*

- *A leader is a dealer in hope.*

- *History is a set of lies agreed upon.*

- *Ability is nothing without opportunity.*

- *Victory belongs to the most persevering.*

- *Impossible is a word to
  be found only in the
  dictionary of fools.*

- *Glory is fleeting, but
  obscurity is forever.*

- *Never interrupt your
  enemy when he is
  making a
  mistake.*

- *If you want a thing done
  well, do it yourself.*

- *An army marches on its
  stomach.*

4-Che Guevara Revolutionary

- *I know you are here to kill me. Shoot, coward, you are only going to kill a man.*

- *If you tremble with indignation at every injustice, then you are a comrade of mine.*

- *The true revolutionary is guided by a great feeling of love. It is impossible to think of a genuine revolutionary lacking this quality.*

- *The revolution is not an apple that falls when it is ripe. You have to make it fall.*

- *We cannot be sure of having something to live for unless we are willing to die for it.*

33

- *Silence is argument
  carried out by other
  means.*

- *Many will call me an
  adventurer - and that I
  am,
   only one of a different
  sort: one of those who
  risks his skin to prove his
  platitudes.*

- *I am not a liberator.
  Liberators do not exist.
  The people liberate
  themselves.*

- *I don't care if I fall as long as someone else picks up my gun and keeps on shooting.*

- *Cruel leaders are replaced only to have new leaders turn cruel.*

5-Fidel Castro
Former Prime Minister
of Cuba

- *A revolution is a struggle to the death between the future and the past.*

- *I find capitalism repugnant. It is filthy, it is gross, it is alienating... because it causes war, hypocrisy and competition.*

- *They talk about the failure of socialism but where is the success of capitalism in Africa, Asia and Latin America?*

- *Men do not shape destiny, Destiny produces the man for the hour.*

- *The revolution is a dictatorship of the exploited against the exploiters.*
- *Capitalism is using its money; we socialists throw it away.*

- *I think that a man should not live beyond the age when he begins to deteriorate, when the flame that lighted the brightest moment of his life has weakened.*

- *No thieves, no traitors, no interventionists! This time the revolution is for real!*

- *The revenues of Cuban state-run companies are used exclusively for the*

*benefit of the people, to
whom they belong.*

6-Yasser arafat

**Former Chairman of the
Palestine Liberation
Organization .**

- *Peace for us means the destruction of Israel. We are preparing for an all-out war, a war which will last for generations.*

- *I come bearing an olive branch in one hand, and the freedom fighter's gun in the other. Do not let the olive branch fall from my hand.*

- In order to obtain the
goal of returning to
Palestine, all of us
sometimes have to grit
our teeth.

- Our law is a Jordanian
law that we inherited,
which applies to both the
West Bank and Gaza, and
sets the death penalty for

- *Whoever thinks of stopping the uprising before it achieves its goals, I will give him ten bullets in the chest.*

7-Julius Caesar

Former Roman dictator

- *It is easier to find men who will volunteer to die, than to find those who are willing to endure pain with patience.*

- *No one is so brave that he is not disturbed by something unexpected.*

- *If you must break the law, do it to seize power: in all other cases observe it.*

8-Alfred noble quote:

- *If I have a thousand ideas and only one turns out to be good, I am satisfied.*

- *Hope is nature's veil for hiding truth's nakedness.*

- *I intend to leave after my death a large fund for the promotion of the peace*

*idea, but I am skeptical
as to its results.*

- *Second to agriculture,
humbug is the biggest
industry of our age.*

9-Ernest Hemingway

American journalist

- *The best way to find out
if you can trust*

somebody is to trust them.

- *The world breaks everyone, and afterward, some are strong at the broken places.*

- *There is nothing to writing. All you do is sit down at a typewriter and bleed.*

- *Always do sober what you said you'd do drunk. That will teach you to keep your mouth shut.*

47

- *But man is not made for defeat. A man can be destroyed but not defeated.*

- *Courage is grace under pressure.*

- *There is no friend as loyal as a book.*

10-William Shakespeare

English poet

- *To thine own self be true, and it must follow, as the night the day, thou canst not then be false to any man.*

- *Brevity is the soul of wit.*

- *The course of true love never did run smooth.*

- *If music be the food of love, play on.*

- *These violent delights have violent ends...*

- *What's in a name? That which we call a rose by any other name would smell as sweet.*

- *Love all, trust a few, do wrong to none.*

11-Pablo Picasso
Spanish painter

- *Every child is an artist. The problem is how to remain an artist once he grows up.*

- *Everything you can imagine is real.*

- *Art washes away from the soul the dust of everyday life.*

- *The purpose of art is washing the dust of daily life off our souls.*

- *Art is a lie that makes us realize truth.*

- *Good artists copy, great artists steal.*

- *Inspiration does exist, but it must find you working.*

- *It takes a long time to become young.*

- *Action is the foundational key to all success.*

- *I am always doing that which I can not do, in order that I may learn how to do it.*

12-Marie Curie
French-Polish physicist

- *Nothing in life is to be feared, it is only to be understood. Now is the time to understand more, so that we may fear less.*

- *Be less curious about people and more curious about ideas.*

- *One never notices what has been done; one can only see what remains to be done.*

- *I was taught that the way of progress was neither swift nor easy.*

- *All my life through, the new sights of Nature made me rejoice like a child.*

- *A scientist in his laboratory is not a mere technician: he is also a child confronting natural phenomena that impress him as though they were fairy tales.*

- *In science, we must be interested in things, not in persons.*

- *I am one of those who think like Nobel, that humanity will draw more good than evil from new discoveries.*

- *I have frequently been questioned, especially by women, of how I could reconcile family life with a scientific career. Well, it has not been easy.*

- *There are sadistic scientists who hurry to hunt down errors instead of establishing the truth.*

13-Johann Wolfgang von Goethe

A german Writer

- *Knowing is not enough; we must apply. Willing is not enough; we must do.*

- *Whatever you can do or dream you can, begin it. Boldness has genius, power, and magic in it.*

- *Few people have the imagination for reality.*

- *None are more hopelessly enslaved than those who falsely believe they are free.*

- The soul that sees beauty may sometimes walk alone.

- Magic is believing in yourself, if you can do that, you can make anything happen.

- As soon as you trust yourself, you will know how to live.

- I call architecture frozen music.

- *Every day we should hear
  at least one little song,
  read one good poem, see
  one exquisite picture,
  and, if possible, speak a
  few sensible words.*

- *Correction does much,
  but encouragement does
  more.*

14-Salvador Dali

Spanish painter

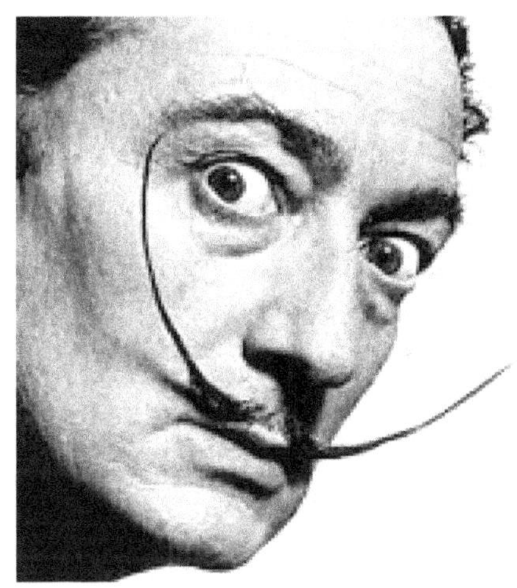

- *I don't do drugs. I am drugs.*

- *Have no fear of perfection - you'll never reach it.*

- *Intelligence without ambition is a bird without wings.*

- *Surrealism is destructive, but it destroys only* **what it considers** *to be shackles limiting our vision.*

- *The only difference between a madman and myself is that I am not mad.*

- *Each morning when I awake, I experience*

*again a supreme pleasure
- that of being Salvador
Dali.*

- *At the age of six I
  wanted to be a cook. At
  seven I wanted to be
  Napoleon. And my
  ambition has been
  growing steadily ever
  since.*

- *Drawing is the honesty of
  the art. There is no
  possibility of cheating. It
  is either good or bad.*

- *Those who do not want
  to imitate anything,
  produce nothing.*

- *I do not paint a portrait
  to look like the subject,
  rather does the person
  grow to look like his
  portrait.*

15-Jean-Jacques Rousseau

Philosopher

- *Man is born free and everywhere he is in chains.*

- *The world of reality has its limits; the world of imagination is boundless.*

- *What wisdom can you find that is greater than kindness?*

- *Absolute silence leads to sadness. It is the image of death.*

- *Those that are most slow in making a promise are the most faithful in the performance of it.*

- *Nature never deceives us; it is we who deceive ourselves.*

- *People who know little are usually great talkers, while men who know much say little.*

- *Happiness: a good bank account, a good cook, and a good digestion.*

- *Childhood is the sleep of reason.*

- *The strongest is never strong enough to be always the master, unless he transforms strength into right, and obedience into duty.*

16-Ludwig van Beethoven Composer

- *Music is a higher revelation than philosophy.*

- *Music is the mediator between the spiritual and the sensual life.*

- *Music should strike fire from the heart of man, and bring tears from the eyes of woman.*

- *Only the pure in heart can make a good soup.*

- *Friends applaud, the comedy is over.*

- *Nothing is more intolerable than to have to admit to yourself your own errors.*

- *I want to seize fate by the throat.*

- *What you are, you are by accident of birth; what I am, I am by myself. There are and will be a thousand princes; there is only one Beethoven.*

17-Adolf Hitler

- *If you tell a big enough lie and tell it frequently enough, it will be believed.*

- *He alone, who owns the youth, gains the future.*

- *Words build bridges into unexplored regions.*

- *Make the lie big, make it simple, keep saying it, and eventually they will believe it.*

- *It is not truth that matters, but victory.*

- *The victor will never be asked if he told the truth.*

- *Humanitarianism is the expression of stupidity and cowardice.*

- *Strength lies not in defence but in attack.*

- *I use emotion for the many and reserve reason for the few.*

- *What luck for rulers that men do not think.*

18-Benito Mussolini

Former Prime Minister of Italy

- *The truth is that men are tired of liberty.*

- *It's good to trust others but, not to do so is much better.*

- *Let us have a dagger between our teeth, a bomb in our hands, and an infinite scorn in our hearts.*

19-Saddam hussein

- *Whoever tries to climb over our fence, we will try to climb over his house.*

- *Who are you and what are you?... I need to know.*

20-Joseph Stalin
Former General Secretary
of the Communist Party of
the Soviet Union

- *Death is the solution to all problems. No man - no problem.*

- *The death of one man is a tragedy. The death of millions is a statistic.*

- *Education is a weapon, whose effect depends on who holds it in his hands and at whom it is aimed.*

- *I believe in one thing only, the power of the human will.*

- *I trust no one, not even myself.*

21-Leonardo da Vinci

Polymath

- *Simplicity is the ultimate sophistication.*

- *Art is never finished, only abandoned.*

- *When once you have tasted flight, you will forever walk the earth with your eyes turned skyward, for there you have been, and there you will always long to return.*

- *Learning never exhausts the mind.*

- *The human foot is a masterpiece of engineering and a work of art.*

- *Painting is poetry that is seen rather than felt, and poetry is painting that is felt rather than seen.*

22-Friedrich Nietzsche

Philosopher

- *He who has a why to live can bear almost any how.*

- *To live is to suffer, to survive is to find some meaning in the suffering.*

- *That which does not kill us makes us stronger.*

- *Without music, life would be a mistake.*

- *One must still have chaos in oneself to be able to give birth to a dancing star.*

- *He who fights with monsters might take care lest he thereby become a monster. And if you gaze for long into an abyss, the abyss gazes also into you.*

- *There are no facts, only interpretations.*

- *I'm not upset that you lied to me, I'm upset that*

*from now on I can't
believe you.*

- *There is always some
madness in love. But
there is also always some
reason in madness.*

- *It is not a lack of love,
but a lack of friendship
that makes unhappy
marriages.*

23-Charlie Chaplin

Comic

- *A day without laughter is a day wasted.*

- *Nothing is permanent in this wicked world - not even our troubles.*

- *Life is a tragedy when seen in close-up, but a comedy in long-shot.*

- *We think too much and feel too little.*

- *You'll never find a rainbow if you're looking down*

- *Failure is unimportant. It takes courage to make a fool of yourself.*

- *I always like walking in the rain, so no one can see me crying.*

- *I remain just one thing, and one thing only -- and that is a clown. It places me on a far higher plane than any politician.*

- *In the end, everything is a gag.*

- *The hate of men will pass, and dictators die, and the power they took from the people will return to the people. And*

24-Henry ford

Ford's Philosophical Quotes

"If money is your hope for independence you will never have it. The only real security that a man will have in this world is a

reserve of knowledge, experience and ability." "If you think you can do a thing or think you can't do a thing, you're right."

25-George Washington

- *It is better to offer no excuse than a bad one.*

- *It is better to be alone than in bad company.*

- *If freedom of speech is taken away, then dumb and silent we may be led, like sheep to the slaughter.*

- *Human happiness and moral duty are inseparably connected.*

- *99% of failures come from people who make excuses.*

26-Muhammad Ali
American professional boxer

- *Float like a butterfly,
  sting like a bee.*

- *Don't count the days,
  make the days count.*

- *He who is not courageous
  enough to take risks will
  accomplish nothing in
  life.*

- *Service to others is the
  rent you pay for your
  room here on earth.*

- *I hated every minute of
  training, but I said, 'Don't*

quit. Suffer now and live
the rest of your life as a
champion.'

- I am the greatest, I said
that even before I knew I
was.

- If you even dream of
beating me you'd better
wake up and apologize.

- It isn't the mountains
ahead to climb that wear

*you out; it's the pebble in
your shoe.*

- *The man who has no
imagination has no
wings.*

- *The fight is won or lost
far away from witnesses
- behind the lines, in the
gym, and out there on
the road, long before I
dance under those lights.*

27-Michael Jordan

American basketball player

- *I've failed over and over and over again in my life and that is why I succeed.*

- *Talent wins games, but teamwork and intelligence wins championships.*

- *I can accept failure, everyone fails at*

something. But I can't accept not trying.

- *Some people want it to happen, some wish it would happen, others make it happen.*

- *One day, you might look up and see me playing the game at 50. Don't laugh. Never say never, because limits, like fears, are often just an illusion.*

- *You have to expect things of yourself before you can do them.*

- *I can accept failure, but I can't accept not trying.*

- *There is no 'i' in team but there is in win.*

- *Just play. Have fun. Enjoy the game.*

- *I've always believed that if you put in the work, the results will come.*

28-Vincent van Gogh
Dutch painter

- *For my part I know nothing with any certainty, but the sight of the stars makes me dream.*

- *I feel that there is nothing more truly artistic than to love people.*

- *I dream of painting and then I paint my dream.*

- *Great things are done by a series of small things brought together.*

- *Love many things, for therein lies the true strength, and whosoever loves much performs much, and can accomplish much, and what is done in love is done well.*

99

- *If you hear a voice within you say 'you cannot paint,' then by all means paint, and that voice will be silenced.*

- *I often think that the night is more alive and more richly colored than the day.*

- *If you truly love Nature, you will find beauty everywhere.*

- *What would life be if we had no courage to attempt anything?*

- *I put my heart and my soul into my work, and have lost my mind in the process.*

29-Albert Einstein

Theoretical physicist

- *Imagination is more important than knowledge.*

- *If you can't explain it simply, you don't understand it well enough.*

- *Two things are infinite: the universe and human*

stupidity; and I'm not sure about the universe.

- *Life is like riding a bicycle. To keep your balance you must keep moving.*

- *No problem can be solved from the same level of consciousness that created it.*

- *The important thing is not to stop questioning.*

*Curiosity has its own
reason for existing.*

- *I have no special talents.
I am only passionately
curious.*

- *Anyone who has never
made a mistake has
never tried anything new.*

- *Logic will get you from A
to B. Imagination will
take you everywhere.*

30-Confucius

Chinese philosopher

- *Wheresoever you go, go with all your heart.*

- *Life is really simple, but men insist on making it complicated.*

- *I hear and I forget. I see and I remember. I do and I understand.*

- *It does not matter how slowly you go so long as you do not stop.*

- *Choose a job you love, and you will never have to work a day in your life.*

- *Only the wisest and stupidest of men never change.*

- *Everything has its beauty, but not everyone sees it.*

- *Never do to others what you would not like them to do to you.*

- *Our greatest glory is not in never falling, but in rising every time we fall.*

31-Mahatma Gandhi

Indian lawyer

- *Happiness is when what you think, what you say, and what you do are in harmony.*

- The weak can never forgive. Forgiveness is the attribute of the strong.

- Where there is love there is life.

- Strength does not come from physical capacity. It comes from an indomitable will.

- In a gentle way, you can shake the world.

- *Earth provides enough to
  satisfy every man's
  needs, but not every
  man's greed.*

- *I will not let anyone walk
  through my mind with
  their dirty feet.*

- *The future depends on
  what we do in the
  present.*

- *A man is but the product of his thoughts; what he thinks, he becomes.*

- *You must not lose faith in humanity. Humanity is an ocean; if a few drops of the ocean are dirty, the ocean does not become dirty.*

32-Omar mukhtar

- *We will never surrender. We win or we die. And don't think it stops there. You will have the next generation to fight; and after the next, the next. As for me, I will live longer than my hangman.*

- *You can only do to me what God decides for me.*

- *From God we come, and unto God we shall return.*

33-Bill Gates

American business magnate

- *Your most unhappy customers are your greatest source of learning.*

- *Success is a lousy teacher. It seduces smart people into thinking they can't lose.*

- *Life is not fair; get used to it.*

- *It's fine to celebrate
  success but it is more
  important to heed the
  lessons of failure.*

- *As we look ahead into the
  next century, leaders will
  be those who empower
  others.*

- *If you can't make it good,
  at least make it look
  good.*

- *The Internet is becoming
  the town square for the*

*global village of
tomorrow.*

- *Technology is just a tool.
In terms of getting the
kids working together
and motivating them, the
teacher is the most
important.*

- *Television is not real life.
In real life people
actually have to leave the
coffee shop and go to
jobs.*

- *Just in terms of allocation
of time resources,*

religion is not very efficient. There's a lot more I could be doing on a Sunday morning.

34-Winston Churchill

Former British Prime Minister

- *Success is not final, failure is not fatal: it is the courage to continue that counts.*

- *If you're going through hell, keep going.*

- *Never, never, never give up.*

- *Success consists of going from failure to failure without loss of enthusiasm.*

117

- *Continuous effort - not strength or intelligence - is the key to unlocking our potential.*

- *We make a living by what we get, but we make a life by what we give.*

- *Never in the field of human conflict was so much owed by so many to so few.*

- *You have enemies? Good. That means you've stood*

*up for something,
sometime in your life.*

- *We shape our buildings; thereafter they shape us.*

- *A pessimist sees the difficulty in every opportunity; an optimist sees the opportunity in every difficulty.*

- *I have conquered an empire but I have not been able to conquer myself. ...*

- *It is my great desire to reform my subjects, and yet I am ashamed to confess that I am unable to reform myself. ...*

- *Destiny may ride with us today, but there is no reason for it to interfere with lunch.*

36-Bill clinton

- *We all do better when we work together. Our differences do matter, but our common humanity matters more.*

- *There is nothing wrong with America that cannot be cured by what is right with America.*

- *When our memories outweigh our dreams.*

- *If you live long enough, you'll make mistakes. But if you learn from them, you'll be a better person. It's how you handle adversity, not how it affects you. The main thing is never quit, never quit, never quit.*

- *We cannot build our own future without*

- *I learned a lot from the stories my uncle, aunts and grandparents told*

*me: that no one is
perfect but most people
are good; that people
can't be judged by their
worst or weakest
moments; that harsh
judgements can make
hypocrites of us all; that
a lot of life is just
showing up and hanging
on; that laughter is often
the best, and sometimes
the only response to
pain.*

*Perhaps most important,
I learned that everyone
has a story – of dreams
and nightmares, hope
and heartache, love and*

loss, courage and fear, sacrifice and selfishness. All my life I've been interested in other people's stories. I wanted to know them, understand them, feel them. When I grew up into politics, I always felt the main point of my work was to people a chance to have better stories.

37-Isaac Newton
Mathematician

- *If I have seen further than others, it is by standing upon the shoulders of giants.*

- *Tact is the knack of making a point without making an enemy.*

- *I can calculate the motion of heavenly bodies, but not the madness of people.*

- *To every action there is always opposed an equal reaction.*

- *Truth is ever to be found in simplicity, and not in the multiplicity and confusion of things.*

- *If I have done the public any service, it is due to my patient thought.*

- *This most beautiful system of the sun, planets and comets, could only proceed from the counsel and dominion of an intelligent and powerful Being.*

- *To myself I am only a child playing on the beach, while vast oceans of truth lie undiscovered before me.*

- *Errors are not in the art but in the artificers.*

- *If I have ever made any valuable discoveries, it has been owing more to patient attention, than to any other talent.*

38-Cristoforo Colombo quotes

- *The sea will grant each man new hope , the sleep brings dreams of home .*

- *You can never cross the ocean unless you have the courage to lose sight of the shore.*

- *So tractable, so peaceable are these people that I swear to your Majesties there is not in the world a better nation. They love their neighbors as themselves, and their discourse is ever sweet and gentle and accompanied with a smile; and though it is*

*true that they are naked,
yet their manners are
decorous and
praiseworthy.*

39-Louis Pasteur

French biologist

- *In the fields of
  observation chance
  favors only the prepared
  mind.*

- *Science knows no
  country, because
  knowledge belongs to
  humanity, and is the
  torch which illuminates
  the world.*

- *Let me tell you the secret
  that has led me to my
  goal. My strength lies
  solely in my tenacity.*

131

- *There are no such things as applied sciences, only applications of science.*

- *Do not let yourself be tainted with a barren skepticism.*

- *When I approach a child, he inspires in me two sentiments; tenderness for what he is, and respect for what he may become.*

40-Galileo Galilei

Astronomer

- *You cannot teach a man
  anything; you can only
  help him find it within
  himself.*

- *All truths are easy to
  understand once they are
  discovered; the point is
  to discover them.*

- *I do not feel obliged to
  believe that the same
  God who has endowed us
  with sense, reason, and*

intellect has intended us to forgo their use.

- *Wine is sunlight, held together by water.*

- *Measure what is measurable, and make measurable what is not so.*

- *In questions of science, the authority of a thousand is not worth the humble reasoning of a single individual.*

- *I have never met a man so ignorant that I couldn't learn something from him.*

- *Mathematics is the language with which God has written the universe.*

- *The sun, with all those planets revolving around it and dependent on it, can still ripen a bunch of grapes as if it had nothing else in the universe to do.*

- *The Bible shows the way
  to go to heaven, not the
  way the heavens go.*

41-Aristotle

Greek philosopher

- *We are what we
  repeatedly do.
  Excellence, then, is not
  an act, but a habit.*

- *The end of labor is to gain leisure.*

- *Pleasure in the job puts perfection in the work.*

- *It is the mark of an educated mind to be able to entertain a thought without accepting it.*

- *The whole is more than the sum of its parts.*

- *Educating the mind without educating the heart is no education at all.*

- *What is a friend? A single soul dwelling in two bodies.*

- *Happiness depends upon ourselves.*

- *The roots of education are bitter, but the fruit is sweet.*

- *Quality is not an act, it is a habit.*

42-Martin Luther

Professor

- *Let the wife make the husband glad to come home, and let him make her sorry to see him leave.*

- *Even if I knew that tomorrow the world would go to pieces, I would still plant my apple tree.*

- *There is no more lovely, friendly and charming relationship, communion*

*or company than a good
marriage.*

- *Every man must do two
things alone; he must do
his own believing and his
own dying.*

- *Anyone who is to find
Christ must first find the
church. How could
anyone know where
Christ is and what faith is
in him unless he knew
where his believers are?*

- *God writes the Gospel
not in the Bible alone,
but also on trees, and in*

*the flowers and clouds
and stars.*

- *Everything that is done in
the world is done by
hope.*

- *Next to the Word of God,
the noble art of music is
the greatest treasure in
the world.*

- *To be a Christian without
prayer is no more
possible than to be alive
without breathing.*

43-the Wright Brothers

"It is possible to fly without motors, but not without knowledge and skill." "The desire to fly is an idea handed down to us by our ancestors who...looked enviously on the birds soaring freely

through space...on the
infinite highway of the
air."

44-Thomas Edison

American inventor

- *I have not failed. I've just found 10,000 ways that won't work.*

- *Our greatest weakness lies in giving up. The most certain way to succeed is always to try just one more time.*

- *Opportunity is missed by most people because it is dressed in overalls and looks like work.*

- *Many of life's failures are people who did not realize how close they were to success when they gave up.*

- *Genius is one percent inspiration and ninety-nine percent perspiration.*
- *If we did all the things we are capable of, we would literally astound ourselves.*

- *The first requisite for success is the ability to apply your physical and mental energies to one problem incessantly without growing weary.*

- *The doctor of the future will give no medicine, but will instruct his patient in the care of the human frame, in diet and in the cause and prevention of disease.*

- *There is no substitute for hard work.*

- *There's a way to do it better - find it.*

45-Plato

Athenian philosopher

- *Love is a serious mental disease.*

- *Be kind, for everyone you meet is fighting a hard battle.*

- *Wise men talk because they have something to say; fools, because they have to say something.*

- *Music is a moral law. It gives soul to the universe, wings to the* mind, flight to the imagination, and charm and gaiety to life and to everything.

- *Only the dead have seen the end of war.*

- *We can easily forgive a child who is afraid of the dark; the real tragedy of life is when men are afraid of the light.*

- One of the penalties for refusing to participate in

politics is that you end up being governed by your inferiors.

- *Man - a being in search of meaning.*

- *At the touch of love everyone becomes a poet.*

- *The beginning is the most important part of the work.*

46-Alexander Graham Bell

Inventor

- *When one door closes another door opens; but we so often look so long and so regretfully upon the closed door, that we do not see the ones which open for us.*

- *Before anything else, preparation is the key to success.*

- *Concentrate all your thoughts upon the work at hand. The sun's rays do not burn until brought to a focus.*

- *Sometimes we stare so long at a door that is closing that we see too late the one that is open.*

- *A man, as a general rule, owes very little to what he is born with – a man*

*is what he makes of
himself.*

- *The most successful men
  in the end are those
  whose success is the
  result of steady
  accretion.*

- *America is a country of
  inventors, and the
  greatest of inventors are
  the newspaper men.*

- *The nation that secures control of the air will ultimately control the world.*

47-Imam " ali ibn abi taleb "

Fourth Caliph of Islam

- *A man's measure is his will.*

- *He who has a thousand friends has not a friend to spare, And he who has one enemy will meet him everywhere.*

- *Do for this life as if you live forever, do for the afterlife as if you die tomorrow.*

- *If you overpower your enemy, then pardon him by way of thankfulness to*

Allah, for being able to subdue him.

- *I was not created to be occupied by eating delicious foods like tied up cattle.*

- *To make one good action succeed another, is the perfection of goodness.*

48-uthman ibn affan

Third caliph of islam

- *Worrying about the dunya is a darkness in the heart, while worrying about akhirah is a light in the heart. ...*

- *Three worldly things have been made dear to me: feeding the hungry, clothing the naked and reading the Qur'an. ...*

- *Acquire wisdom from the story of those who have already passed.*

- *Allah the Exalted loves him who forgoes worldly life, the Angels love him who rejects the vices, and the Muslims love him who gives up greediness in respect of the Muslims.*

49-Umar Ibn Al-Khattab
The second caliph in Islam

- *The best way to defeat someone is to beat him at politeness.*

- *Do not grieve over what has passed unless it makes you work harder for what is about to come.*

- *Whosoever shows you your faults is your friend. Those that pay you lip service in praise are your executioners*

- *I have never regretted my silence, as for my speech I've regretted it many times.*

- *The less attachment to the world. The easier your life.*
- *Remind yourselves of God, for it is a cure. Do not remind yourselves of*

the people, for it is a
disease.

- *A man should be like a
child with his wife, but if
she needs him, he should
act like a man.*

- *The most beloved of
people to me is he that
points out my flaws to
me.*

- *Learn the Arabic
language; it will sharpen
your wisdom.*

- *Sit with those who have sinned and repented for they have the softest of hearts.*

- *No amount of guilt can change the past and no amount of worrying can change the future.*

- *Sometimes the people with the worst past, create the best future.*
- *Get used to a rough life, for luxury does not last forever.*

162

- *My heart is at ease
  knowing that what was
  meant for me will never
  miss me and that what
  misses me was never
  meant for me.*

- *To be alone you avoid
  bad company. But to
  have a true friend is
  better than being alone.*

- *Be dignified, honest, and
  truthful.*

- *Let not your love become attachment, nor your hate become destruction.*

- *To speak less is wisdom, to eat less is healthy, and to mingle less with the people is safe and serene.*

- *The women are not a garment you wear and undress however you like. They are honored and have their rights.*

- *Doing good for a good done to you is simply repayment, whereas*

doing good for an evil
done to you is a
tremendous virtue.

- *Don't forget your own
self while preaching to
others.*

- *Acquire knowledge and
teach it to people.*

- *The wisest man is he who
can account for his
actions.*

- *I wish you knew what I
have in my heart for you,*

but there is no way for you to know except by my actions.

- *Do not put off today's work for tomorrow.*

- *Patience is a pillar of faith.*

- *May God bless the man who says less and does more.*

50-Abu baker siddiq
The first caliph in
Islam

- *Without knowledge action is useless and knowledge without action is futile.*

- *Knowledge is the life of the mind.*

- *The more knowledge you have, the greater will be your fear of Allah.*

- *It is a matter of shame that in the morning the birds should be awake earlier than you.*

- *Run away from greatness and greatness will follow you.*

- *If you expect the blessings of God, be kind to His people.*

- *The greatest truth is honesty, and the greatest falsehood is dishonesty.*

- *He who avoids complaint invites happiness.*

The Three Greatest Characters in History

Prophet Moses

- *You shall not steal, nor deal falsely, nor lie to one another.*

- *See, I have set before you this day life and good, death and evil... I have set before you life and death, blessing and curse; therefore choose life.*

Prophet Isaiah " Jesus "

- *Fear not; you will no longer live in shame. Don't be afraid; there is no more disgrace for you.*

- *For your Creator will be your husband; the Lord of Heaven's Armies is his name!*

Prophet Muhammad ﷺ

Prophet of islam

- *Kindness is a mark of faith, and whoever has not kindness has not faith.*

- *Four things support the world: the learning of the wise, the justice of the great, the prayers of the good, and the valor of the brave.*

- *The ink of the scholar is
  more sacred than the
  blood of the martyr.*

- *None of you truly
  believes until he wishes
  for his brother what he
  wishes for himself.*

- *To overcome evil with
  good is good, to resist
  evil by evil is evil.*

Success stories of some famous personalities

Jeff Bezos | From a geek to an entrepreneur heading towards world domination

It wasn't until he turned 10, Bezos found out that he had a stepfather. It had been years since his biological father left, but that didn't stop him from becoming a billionaire, in fact, that was only the beginning of his journey to get to the top.Jeff Bezos Success Story youngWhile spending summers in Texas, he was introduced to the space industry where his grandfather worked and so he became a role model for little Jeff, who dreamed of achieving greatness. As a child, Bezos had broad interests, particularly in science. One time, he converted his parent's garage into a science laboratory where he made things like cooking contraptions from an

umbrella or an alarm
system using parts from
Radio shack. He was always
very bookish which was
why his mother enrolled
him into the gifted kids
program and that led him
to become a valedictorian
in high school. So off he set
to Princeton to study
physics only to realize his
brain wasn't wired to
calculate momentum and
inertia. Thus, he switched
majors and graduated in
computer science and
electrical engineering.

He finally stepped into the
real world as he started a
job in New York for a high
tech startup in the financial
industry. When he failed to
raise money for a fax
newsletter startup he
looked for another
business, and as luck would
have it ended up with a job
at Wall Street. He knew it
wouldn't be long when
internet commerce would
be introduced and he came
up with the idea for an
"everything store" where
online transactions would
be at your fingertips. After
talking to his bosses and

177

telling them his idea, they encouraged him but told him "it was better off left to someone who doesn't already have a good job".

Determined, Bezos quit his job and shifted to Seattle where he went on to start the company anyway. Initially he was going to call the company "Cadabra" because it had magical connotations but eventually settled on Amazon, based on the largest river in the world. And let's just say his road to success wasn't all butterflies and rainbows.

His first item to be sold were books which he wouldn't physically buy but bought it when the customers did. He started working in his garage with his wife and two programmers, initially, investing all his money. Starting a remarkable journey ahead, Bezos launched Amazon officially.Jeff Bezos Success Story house

He somehow raised a staggering 1M from colleagues, family and investors. He started packing hundreds of books by hand but with every step he took forward he was tackled by his competitors, who often threatened to crush him. It was only when he met Larry Page and Sergey Brin, founders of Google, and invested in them that he started making profits. During the first 3 years, people thought he would fail making fun of amazon, calling it "amazon.bomb", "amazon.toast", "amazon.con" but Bezos went on to build the world's most consumer centric company – inspired by founder of Sony (Masaru Ibuka).

It took amazon more than 6 years, but in 2001 they posted their first quarterly profits and now Amazon is the world's largest ecommerce company with a revenue of over 34.2 billion and more than a billion in profit (2010). Of course there were downfalls, Bezos lost hundreds of millions when his investments went bust (pets.com, gear.com) but like a good sport he got back up and recovered.

In an interview he once said, "I didn't think I'd regret trying and failing and I suspected I would always be haunted by a decision to not try at all", and that led him to become the 5th richest man in the world.

Bill Gates Success Story

Bill Gates was born on
October 28, 1955 in Seattle in
a family having rich business,
political and community
service background. His
great-grandfather was a state
legislator and a mayor, his
grandfather was vice
president of national bank
and his father was a lawyer.

Bill believed in achieving his
goals through hard work. He
also believes that if you are
intelligent and know how to
use your intelligence, you can
reach your goals and targets.
From his early days Bill was
ambitious, competitive and

intelligent. These qualities helped him to attain great position in the profession he chose also Bill was deemed by his peers and his teachers as the smartest kid on campus; Bill's parents came to know their son's intelligence and decided to enroll him in a private school, known for its intense academic environment. That was the most important decision in Bill Gate's life where he was first introduced to computers. Bill Gates and his friends were very much interested in computer and formed "Programmers Group" in late 1968. Being in this group, they found a new way to apply their computer skill in university of Washington. In the next year, they got their first opportunity in Information Sciences Inc. in which they were selected as programmers. ISI (Information Sciences Inc.) agreed to give them royalties, whenever it made money from any of the group's program. As a result of the business deal signed with Information Sciences Inc., the group also became a legal business.

Bill Gates and his close friend Allen formed a new company of their own, Traf-O-Data. They developed a small computer to measure traffic flow. From this project they earned around $20,000. The era of Traf-O-Data came to an end when Gates left the college. Upon graduating from Lakeside Bill enrolled in Harvard University in 1973, one of the best universities in the country, He didn't know what to do, so he enrolled his name for pre-law. He took the standard freshman courses with the exception of signing up for one of Harvard's toughest mathematics courses. He did well over there, but he couldn't find it interesting too. He spent many long nights in front of the school's computer and the next day asleep in class. After leaving school, he almost lost himself from the world of computers. Gates and his friend Paul Allen remained in close contact even though they were away from school. They would often discuss new ideas for future projects and the possibility of starting a business one fine day. At the end of Bill's first year, Allen came close to him so that they could follow some of their ideas. That summer they got job in Honeywell. Allen kept on pushing Bill for opening a new software company.

Within a year, Bill Gates dropped out from Harvard. Then he formed Microsoft. Microsoft's vision is "A computer on every desk and Microsoft software on every computer". Bill is a visionary person and works very hard to achieve his vision. His belief in high intelligence and hard work has put him where he is today. He does not believe in mere luck or God's grace, but just hard work and competitiveness. Bill's Microsoft is good competition for other software companies and he will continue to stomp out (challenge) the competition until he dies. He likes to play the game of Risk and the game of world domination. His beliefs are so powerful, which have helped him increase his wealth and his monopoly in the industry.

Bill Gates is not a greedy person. In fact, he is quite giving person when it comes to computers, internet and

189

any kind of funding. Some
years back, he visited
Chicago's Einstein Elementary
School and announced grants
benefiting Chicago's schools
and museums where he
donated a total of $110,000,
a bunch of computers, and
provided internet connectivity
to number of schools.
Secondly, Bill Gates donated
38 million dollars for the
building of a computer
institute at Stanford
University.

Thomas Edison success story

Failure happens. It happens all the time, to everyone, and sometimes can have a bad effect on us depending on the way we react to it.

Failure, like many other things, is something we have got used to through the years. To some it has become a lifestyle, an ingrained habit

we just can't break if we don't
have the right mindset.

The greatest example, when
it comes down to failure, is
the American inventor
Thomas Edison.
He failed more than 10,000
times (I am still amazed at
that number!) before he
created the light bulb.

That makes him a true
example of perseverance.

What helped him was
understanding a few things –
defining success and failure,
realizing the inevitable

connection between them,
never giving up, working
hard, believing in himself and
his ideas.

Of course, in many situations
things looked so hopeless and
pointless that the average
person would have given up
on his work. But not him.

Many people told him that he
is wasting his time, his faith
and confidence were
sometimes on the verge of
being gone, but he
succeeded. Many times.

The fruits of his labor were 1093 patents, including the bulb, the phonograph, the motion picture camera, the printing telegraph apparatus, typewriting machines, telephones and many other things we can't live without today.

If it wasn't for him and other great people in the history – leaders, scientists, businessmen, inventors and so on – we wouldn't have electricity, running water, cars, TV, computers and all the other things that make our life comfortable and easy.

Imagine what the world would be like if every one of them just gave up on his ideas to try something new, to change the world and help people. Just imagine...

Failure must be understood perfectly in order for us to be successful and follow our dreams.

So let's analyze Thomas Edison's way of thinking by taking a look at his words.

1. " I have not failed. I've just found 10,000 ways that won't work."

He accepts failure. He finds its positive side and realizes that it is something as normal as success. And thus we need to learn how to fail before we learn how to succeed.

2. "Our greatest weakness lies in giving up. The most certain way to succeed is always to try just one more time."

Giving up is what stopped many people from becoming

more, from achieving
greatness and changing the
world.

Giving up is the state in which
our mind shows the white
flag, in which it's easier for us
not to move on, not to try
one more time and to just
listen to the naysayers.

But we can all overcome that
point. We can keep believing
because everything around us
is an example of what
happens if someone keeps
pushing.

197

The answer is to just try one more time.

Do it without thinking too much, without analyzing the situation, without listening to the others and without fearing the chance of failing again.

3. "Genius is one percent inspiration and ninety-nine percent perspiration."

Remember that no matter what you have achieved so far, no matter how experienced or educated you

are and no matter where you
come from and where you're
going, you can get what you
want by working hard.

Hard work combined with
focus will always have results.
So perspire and success will
come

4. "There's a way to do it
better – find it."

As human beings we can
change our body and mind
however we want. It's not
easy – it never is, but once
we've done it right, nothing

will be able to stand in our
way.

Whatever we do, there is
always a chance to do it
better.

We are born to thrive,
improve and evolve and that
is why we have to try again
and again if we really want
something.

5.” When I have fully decided
that a result is worth getting I
go ahead of it and make trial
after trial until it comes.”

You need to know whether
your idea is worth it or not.
And if it is – never give up on
it until you succeed.

Create it in your mind first,
reach success there before
you actually do it.

And then, after putting in
enough effort, after
dedicating time and energy,
you will start seeing results.
You will see your idea in
reality and the moment you
see someone using what
you've invented and how it
helps people live better – you

will know that all the sweat
was worth it.

6. "We don't know a millionth
of one percent about
anything."

Realize and accept how much
you don't know and how more
you have to learn.

Every time you try you can
fail because of not knowing
how to do it right. But that
can be changed.

You can learn new things
every day and do your best to
become professional in your

field. Then you will know exactly what to do and how to do it and this time failure won't be an option.

7. "It is astonishing what an effort it seems to be for many people to put their brains definitely and systematically to work."

Focus!

Only a concentrated man can work adequately.
Only a concentrated mind can think of a thousand ways to do one thing and each one of them can be brilliant.

You may be able to work for
days without resting, but you
are wasting your time if you
don't stay focused.
And sometimes only 60
minutes of concentration a
day can bring the best
results.

Have these statements in
mind next time you try to do
something. Remember that
failure is a state of mind, just
like success, and that makes
it something we can control.

Without failure, we can't
succeed. They are connected

in a way we can understand
only if we accept the former
in order to reach the latter.

So here is a summary of the
important lessons Thomas
Edison wants every
generation to learn:

Accept failure;
Never give up;
Work hard;
Find a better way to do it;
Try until you succeed;
Learn and improve so that
you don't fail next time;
Stay focused.

Henry ford success story

Henry Ford is one of the most renowned entrepreneurs in history. He optimized transportation and forever changed the United States automobile industry. His innovative manufacturing process produced low-cost, reliable vehicles, while simultaneously keeping his workers well-paid and loyal.

Before his success, however, Ford encountered failure during initial production of his first automobile. His investors got cold feet over Ford's meticulousness, and he was unable to find solid financial backing for the automobile in his first two ventures. Nonetheless, Ford used the lessons from these failures to instruct his future success as an inventor and a businessman.

William H. Murphy
Folds...Twice

Once Ford created the Quadricycle, an automobile prototype, he needed funding to start work on enhancing it.

Capital was difficult to attain, however, and in the late 1800s no one had established a standard business model for the automobile industry. Ford convinced William H. Murphy, a Detroit businessman, to back his automobile production. The Detroit Automobile Company resulted from this union, but problems arose shortly after its creation. In 1901, a year and a half after the company began operations, Murphy and the shareholders got restless. Ford wanted to create the perfect automobile design, but the board saw little results. Soon after, they dissolved the company.

Ford recalibrated his efforts after his first failure. He realized that his previous automobile design depended on serving numerous consumer needs. He convinced Murphy to give him a second chance, a rare occurrence in the early 20th century. However, their second venture, the Henry Ford Company, stumbled from the start. Ford felt that Murphy pressured him to prepare the automobile for production and set unrealistic

expectations from the
beginning. Shortly after
Murphy brought in an outside
manager to supervise Ford's
process, Ford left the
company and everyone wrote
him off.

These two failures could have
been career-ending, but Ford
continued. Several years after
the second parting with
Murphy, Ford met Alexander
Malcomson, a coal magnate
with a risk-taking spirit like
Ford. Malcomson gave Ford
full control over his
production, and the company

introduced the Model A in
1904.

For Henry Ford, failure did not
hinder innovation, but served
as the impetus to hone his
vision for a technology that
would ultimately transform
the world.

211

Muhammad ali success story

Born in January 17, 1942
American professional boxer
Muhammad Ali is widely
regarded as one of the most
significant and celebrated
sports figures of the 20th
century. He won a gold medal
in the 1960 Summer
Olympics in Rome and was
the first three-time
heavyweight boxing champion

of the world. But how did he become "The Greatest"?

Beginning

Despite his talent to creating amazing poems before the fights, he hated to read. In fact, Ali was dyslexic, and barely graduated from high school. "He graduated 376 out of a class of 391. " – CBS News. 'I never said I was the smartest, I said I was the greatest,' – as Muhammad said.

When he was 12 years old someone stole his bicycle. Furious, Muhammad Ali went to report the crime to police officer Joe Martin, who was also a boxing coach at the Columbia Gym. When Muhammad Ali said he wanted to beat up the person who stole his bike, Martin told him that he should probably learn to fight first. A few days later he began boxing training at Martin's gym. Soon Ali began taking his diet seriously avoiding alcohol, cigarettes and the junk food he loved.

Career

Ali became professional in 1960. He had won 29 matches in a row without losing even one. When he won the World Heavyweight Title from Sony Liston in 1964 he was the youngest person to take the title. The day after winning the championship, he changed his name from Cassius Clay and announced his conversion to Islam. The public was not happy.

"I ain't got no quarrel with them Viet Cong."

– Muhammad Ali

Because of his religious beliefs in 1960 Ali refused to be inducted into the armed forces. Muhammad Ali was banned from boxing and stripped of his heavyweight title. He was also charged of five years in prison which meant his boxing career was almost over.

Comeback

After victory in federal court Ali returned to the ring in 1970 with a win over Jerry Quarry. The fight went the full 15 rounds, with both fighters still standing at the end but by unanimously decision Ali lost making the fight his first professional defeat. But in 1974, Ali came back to defeat Joe Frazier after a tough climb to the top.

In 1974 Ali got chance to fight for Heavyweight Title with George Foreman. Ali was much slower and older than he used to while Foreman was considered to be unbeatable. For the second time But Ali made history when he won that fight in eight-round and for the second time become the heavyweight champion of the world.

In 1978, Muhammad Ali was extremely surprised when novice boxer Leon Spinks beat him. Ali admitted that he was not at his best and vowed to win back the title in a rematch. He won and became the first person to win the Heavyweight title three times.

Philanthropy and Parkinson's Syndrome

Muhammad Ali finished his career with 56 wins (37 by KO) and 5 losses.Unfortunately, all of these fights took a toll on Muhammad Ali's body. After suffering increasingly slurred speech, shaking hands, and over-tiredness, Muhammad Ali was diagnosed with Parkinson's syndrome in 1984.

In his retirement, Ali devoted much of his time to philanthropy also supported the Special Olympics and the Make-A-Wish Foundation. "Ali traveled to numerous countries, including Mexico and Morocco, to help out those in need. In 1998, he was chosen to be a United Nations Messenger of Peace because of his work in developing nations."

Muhammad Ali considered one of the greatest heavyweights of all time by boxing commentators and historians passed away on the evening of June 3, 2016, at a Phoenix, Arizona facility.

Michael Jordan success story

Michael Jordan needs no introduction. Something of a legend for turning failure into success, he is the author of

the longest quote on my
company's failure wall —
which was tricky to paint but
worth the extra effort:

I've missed more than 9,000
shots in my career. I've lost
almost 300 games. Twenty-
six times, I've been trusted to
take the game-winning shot
and missed. I've failed over
and over and over again in
my life. And that is why I
succeed.

Most of us don't fail or
succeed in the glare of a
national spotlight, much less

do it thousands of times, with
analysts endlessly critiquing
every move. Perhaps that's
why people love sports: they
provide a black and white
analogy for the gray backdrop
of life. The ball is in or it's
out, the basket is made or
missed, the game is won or
lost. Watching our favorite
stars pull through when the
chips are down inspires us to
do the same in our own lives.
And no one has inspired more
sports fans, young and old
alike, than Michael Jordan.

The story of Michael Jordan
not making his high school

team has been told and retold, but continues to inspire with each retelling. In 1978, sophomore Michael Jordan tried out for the varsity basketball team at Laney High School. When the list was posted, Jordan's name wasn't on it. Instead, he was asked to play on the junior varsity team.

The reasoning behind the choice wasn't that Jordan didn't have enough talent or hadn't already distinguished himself as an outstanding basketball player. Rather, it came down to seniority, size, and a strategic decision: The varsity team already had eleven seniors and three juniors. That left space for only one more player, and the coaches chose another sophomore, Jordan's friend Leroy Smith. Smith was not as good as Jordan but he added size to the team, as he was 6'6" compared to Jordan's diminutive 5'10". What's more, the coaches knew that if Jordan had been chosen for the varsity team, he would play only when needed as a substitute for the more senior varsity players. On the junior varsity team he would get more playing time and a chance to truly develop.

It was a perfectly logical choice for the coaches to assign Jordan to the junior varsity team for his sophomore year. But 15-year-old Jordan was devastated when the list was posted without his name. In his mind, it was the ultimate defeat, the ultimate failure. "I went to my room and I closed the door and I cried. For a while I couldn't stop. Even though there was no one else home at the time, I kept the door shut. It was important to me that no one hear me or see me." Jordan was heartbroken and ready to give up the sport altogether until his mother convinced him otherwise.

His relentless drive would lead him to break numerous records and become the most decorated player in the history of the NBA...he's credited with dramatically increasing the popularity of basketball both in the United States and internationally, and inspiring the next generation of basketball players...

227

After picking himself up off the floor, Jordan did what champions do. He let his failure and disappointment drive him to be better. He played on the junior varsity team, and he worked himself to the limit. "Whenever I was working out and got tired and figured I ought to stop, I'd close my eyes and see that list in the locker room without my name on it, and that usually got me going again."

It became a pattern throughout Jordan's life that a disappointment or setback resulted in a redoubling of effort. High school rival player Kenny Gattison, who led his team to beat Jordan's team for the high school state championship, put it this way: "You got to understand what fuels that guy, what makes him great. For most people the pain of loss is temporary. [Jordan] took that loss and held on to it. It's a part of what made him."

For most people, public failure becomes public humiliation, and that leads to retreat. Fear of public speaking is a good example. Few people are psychologically afraid of speaking their mind and even fewer have physical speech impediments preventing them from doing so. Yet glossophobia, the technical term for speech anxiety, is consistently ranked among the most prevalent mental disorders, with a reputed 75% of the world's population experiencing some degree of anxiety around public speaking. Our fears have little to do with speaking, of course, and far more to do with the perceived impact and reaction that our audience may have. But for Jordan and elite performers like him, the fear of failure and public ridicule is transformed into a drive for success.

The pattern of defeat followed by success would follow Jordan to the University of North Carolina and later to the NBA. His relentless drive would lead him to break numerous records and become the most decorated player in the history of the NBA. What's more, he's credited with dramatically increasing the popularity of basketball both in the United States and internationally, and inspiring the next generation of basketball players including Lebron James, Dwyane Wade, and Kobe Bryant. You can't think of the word "champion" without thinking of Michael Jordan, and there's no better proof that failure is simply a stepping stone to success.

Michael Jordan faced another formidable challenge decades later, when he became the owner of the NBA basketball franchise, the Charlotte Bobcats. Jordan had been a minority owner since 2006 but bought the majority stake from Bob Johnson in 2010. At the time, the business was hemorrhaging, so Jordan used his own money to cover the significant operating losses the team was experiencing.

The first season was lackluster but things got worse. In the 2011-2012 season, the team earned a mere 7 wins alongside 59 losses – the worst record of any team ever in the history of the NBA.

In addition to—or maybe because of—their disastrous

record, the Bobcats had poor community support. The Bobcats brand was synonymous with disappointment, despite having one of the best basketball brands of all time at the helm—Michael Jordan himself.

But after the 2012-2013 season came to a close, Jordan started to turn things around. First, he brought in former Lakers assistant coach Steve Clifford to replace Mike Dunlap. In a change every bit as important as the new coach, Jordan agreed to

remove himself from the
process of managing the
team's operations.

Instead, Jordan focused on
what Jordan can do better
than anyone else: revitalizing
the brand. He applied for and
received permission to
change the team name to the
Charlotte Hornets. Jordan
himself became more
involved in community events
and forged a connection
between the team and the
city.

The changes paid off. The team finished the 2013-2014 season with a winning record of 43-39, the second best year in the history of the franchise. They even made it to the playoffs. At the same time, ticket and merchandise sales skyrocketed and public opinion improved dramatically. The team was well on its way to making both a comeback and a profit.

Most of us look to successful people and assume they can do anything because of their past successes. The old joke about asking your doctor for stock tips comes to mind, as if just because you can cure an illness, you have wisdom about everything. Doctors don't make great stockbrokers, brain surgeons are horrible rocket scientists, CEOs aren't usually exceptional cooks, and basketball stars are rarely great baseball players (you can ask Jordan about that last one as well). Experience and knowledge are only valuable where applicable.

This mindset doesn't just fog our external lenses, it also blurs how we see ourselves.

It is often hard for successful people to admit that they won't be good at something new. In Jordan's case, his basketball skills didn't translate into basketball management. It took some time, but Jordan certainly deserves credit for acknowledging what wasn't working and trying new things until he hit on a winning combination. He gave up managing and focused on marketing, a skill he was uniquely qualified for. For Jordan, that became the recipe for success:

It's harder than most people think. Some people have been in this business a lot longer and still haven't put together a sustainable, successful scenario. When you make bad decisions, you learn from that and move forward. I think I'm better in that sense. I've experienced all of the different valleys and lows about ownership and the success of businesses. Does that constitute me being a better owner? Then I guess I am.

Hard, yes, but flexing a new muscle is also exhilarating,

especially when you eventually succeed. As Jordan puts it, "…it's been fun. It's been hard, but I've had fun doing it."

Isaac Newton story

Legend has it that a young Isaac Newton was sitting under an apple tree when he was bonked on the head by a falling piece of fruit, a 17th-century "aha moment" that prompted him to suddenly come up with his law of gravity. In reality, things didn't go down quite like that. Newton, the son of a farmer, was born in 1642 near Grantham, England, and entered Cambridge University in 1661. Four years later, following an outbreak of the bubonic plague, the school temporarily closed, forcing Newton to move back to his childhood home, Woolsthorpe Manor. It was during this period at Woolsthorpe (Newton returned to Cambridge in 1667) that he was in the orchard there and witnessed an apple drop from a tree. There's no evidence to suggest the fruit actually landed on his head, but Newton's observation caused him to ponder why apples always fall straight to the ground (rather than sideways or upward) and helped inspired him to eventually develop his law of universal gravitation. In 1687, Newton first published this principle, which states that every body in the universe is attracted to every other body with a force that is directly proportional to the product of their masses and inversely proportional to the square of the distance between them, in his landmark work the "Principia," which also features his three laws of motion.

In 1726, Newton shared the apple anecdote with William Stukeley, who included it in a biography, "Memoirs of Sir

Isaac Newton's Life,"
published in 1752. According
to Stukeley, "After dinner, the
weather being warm, we went
into the garden, & drank the
under the shade of some
apple trees… he told me, he
was just in the same
situation, as when formerly,
the notion of gravitation came
into his mind…. occasion'd by
the fall of an apple, as he sat
in a contemplative mood."

The esteemed mathematician
and physicist died in 1727
and was buried at
Westminster Abbey. His
famous apple tree continues

to grow at Woolsthorpe
Manor.

Marie curie story

In 1903 Madame Curie became the first woman to win a Nobel Prize when she shared one half of the award in physics for the discovery of radioactivity with her husband Pierre. In 1910 she published her fundamental treatise on Radioactivity. The other half was awarded to Henry Becquerel. In 1911 she multiplied her earlier feat by being the sole winner of the Nobel Prize in chemistry for the discovery of Polonium and

Radium, thus becoming the
only person to be awarded
the elusive medal in multiple
sciences.

Marie Curie's exhaustive body
of work is studded with
international medals, awards
and other notable
recognitions. However, even
after two Nobels under her
belt, she was denied many an
honours simply for being a
woman. These went to men
who were significantly less
qualified than her. Case in
point is when she was
defeated by a mere two votes
to succeed the position left

247

vacant by Gernez in the French Academy of Sciences. This happened in 1911, the very year she won her second Nobel Prize in chemistry!

But the remarkable woman did not let this deter her work. She went on to help found the famous Radium Institute of the University of Paris in 1914. She had already become the first woman to teach at Sorbonne in 1906, though this came about via tragic circumstances. Pierre Curie was killed in a carriage accident while crossing the street in April 19th 1906, and it was his professorship that she succeeded. Marie Curie was determined to devoting her life to the work that she and her husband had partnered together so successfully. With the advent of World War I she became fanatically immersed in finding practical medical applications for radioactivity.

Her daughter Irene Curie was now an integral part of her research team. The Radium Institute became the hub of pioneering nuclear physics and chemistry research. The development of X Radiography was her most notable accomplishment this period. From 1921 onwards she travelled all over the world, giving speeches and demonstrating her work. The American President Warren Harding presented her with one gram of radium, in recognition of her immense contribution to science, when she journeyed to USA.

The damaging effects of radium were not known when Marie Curie was working with them. She carried radioactive isotopes in her pocket, kept

samples in her desk drawers
and in general was exposed
to every harmful aspect of it
in the course of her research.
She was not the only one.
Manufacturers assumed that
something as wondrous as
radioactivity had to be full of
benefits for the human kind.
Radioactive substances were
put in toothpastes, laxatives
and all manner of household
goods and products. Hotels
and resorts proudly
advertised their therapeutic
radioactive mineral springs.
Madame Curie contracted
Leukemia from her lifelong
exposure to radioactive

substances and died in 1934. The mal-effects of radiation are so deadly that all her original research papers and stationery, even her personal items like clothing and cookbooks, are very dangerous to touch. Her lab books are preserved in lead lined boxes. Those wishing to handle them have to don layers of protective clothing to be permitted even in the vicinity of the Curie sanctuary.

Thank you for reading, I hope this book will change many people's life

Mohammad Adeeb

253